Fact Finders®

HUMANS AND OUR PLANET

HUMANS AND THE HYDROSPHERE

Protecting Earth's water sources

Ava Sawyer

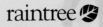

raintree

a Capstone company — publishers for children

Raintree is an imprint of Capstone Global Library Limited, a company incorporated in England and Wales having its registered office at 264 Banbury Road, Oxford, OX2 7DY – Registered company number: 6695582

www.raintree.co.uk
myorders@raintree.co.uk

Edited by Nikki Potts
Designed by Philippa Jenkins
Original illustrations © Capstone Global Library Limited 2017
Picture research by Jo Miller
Production by Kathy McColley
Originated by Capstone Global Library Limited
Printed and bound in China

ISBN 978-1-4747-4374-7
21 20 19 18 17
10 9 8 7 6 5 4 3 2 1

British Library Cataloguing in Publication Data
A full catalogue record for this book is available from the British Library.

Acknowledgements
We would like to thank the following for permission to reproduce photographs: Alamy: Ronald Karpilo, 25; Shutterstock: Action Sports Photography, 21, Ammit Jack, 4, Angelo Giampiccolo, 12, Annzee, 11, AuntSpray, 15, B Brown, 18, corbac40, 24, Corepics VOF, 23 (top), CRSHELARE, 16, DoublePHOTO studio, 13, khwanchai, 7, Maciej Bledowski, 20, marekuliasz, 14, Matyas Rehak, 8, Michaelpuche, 10, Narin Nonthamand, 26–27, OPIS Zagreb, 5, Philip Pilosian, 17, Photodiem, cover, Rawpixel.com, throughout (background), Signature Message, 22-23, smereka, 9, Sue Burton PhotographyLtd, 19, wickerwood, 6

Every effort has been made to contact copyright holders of material reproduced in this book. Any omissions will be rectified in subsequent printings if notice is given to the publisher.

All the internet addresses (URLs) given in this book were valid at the time of going to press. However, due to the dynamic nature of the internet, some addresses may have changed, or sites may have changed or ceased to exist since publication. While the author and publisher regret any inconvenience this may cause readers, no responsibility for any such changes can be accepted by either the author or the publisher.

CONTENTS

WHAT IS THE HYDROSPHERE?

Earth is very different from other planets. Water covers most of our planet. The hydrosphere includes all of the water found on Earth. Water is on the surface, underground, in the air and a part of every living thing. Water can be in the form of a liquid, solid or gas. Life on Earth would not be possible without water.

Rivers, lakes, oceans, streams and glaciers are all part of the hydrosphere.

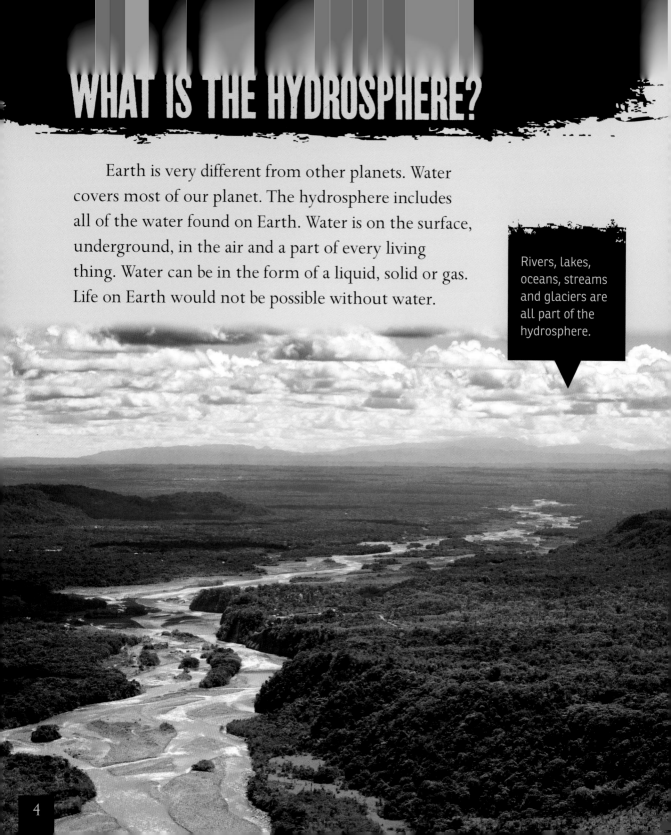

Earth has five oceans: Pacific, Atlantic, Indian, Southern and Arctic.

Earth's temperature allows most of the hydrosphere to be in liquid form. However, more than 97 per cent of it is salt water. Salt water is unusable by most land animals, including humans. Oceans are large bodies of salt water. They cover more than 70 per cent of Earth and hold most of the planet's water. Oceans are the biggest part of the hydrosphere.

Fresh water is found either frozen, underground or on Earth's surface in ponds, streams, rivers and lakes.

Oceans

The movement of the ocean is also a big part of the hydrosphere. Tides, currents and waves move and mix the water. They help control Earth's climate while carrying life to every corner of the world. Tides affect the movement of the entire ocean. They are long waves that follow the moon's gravity. Tides cause shoreline sea levels to rise and fall twice every day.

The **water cycle** moves water within the hydrosphere. Water changes form throughout the cycle. The sun's energy **evaporates** surface water, mostly from the oceans. The water becomes vapour and forms clouds. It then condenses and falls back to Earth as rain or snow. Falling water — precipitation — shapes continents, fills lakes and forms rivers. Water collects in these **reservoirs** and begins the cycle all over again. It is always moving, changing and being reused all around our planet.

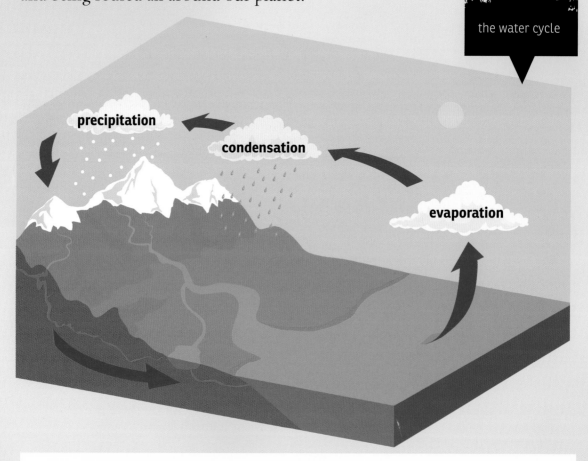

the water cycle

precipitation

condensation

evaporation

water cycle how water changes as it travels around the world and moves between the ground and the air

evaporate to change from a liquid into a vapour or gas

reservoir a natural or artificial holding area for storing large amounts of water

As water moves through the water cycle, it changes phases. It can change between liquid, gas and solid.

Earth's hydrosphere is a closed system. No water is added to or subtracted from it. The amount of water on Earth does not change over time. Today's water is the same water that existed during the time of the dinosaurs. Water is constantly in motion, being transformed and reused all over the planet. Water helps people, plants and animals to survive. However, human activities are threatening the hydrosphere and the future of life on Earth.

A closed system

Because the water cycle circulates water from the surface of Earth to the atmosphere and back, the water supply seems to constantly renew itself. Still, rubbish and pollution has made some fresh water undrinkable. Turning salt water into drinking water is complicated and expensive. In addition, pollution threatens groundwater supplies. Groundwater is the main source of fresh water for much of the world's population. Contaminated groundwater can lead to a wide range of health problems. So even though the amount of water on Earth does not change, it is still important to conserve this resource.

PEOPLE AND THE HYDROSPHERE

Water can be a source of entertainment. Many seek out sources of water for weekend activities. People travel to oceans, lakes and rivers to relax and play. Public parks are often found near large bodies of water. People enjoy fishing, swimming, sailing, snorkelling, scuba diving, kayaking, canoeing, paddle boarding and water skiing. Many enjoy ice skating in the winter. People also run, hike, bike, picnic and camp around lakes. It is nice to enjoy water and the outdoors. It is also important to take care of them.

People of all ages snorkel on a coral reef in Sri Lanka.

People are changing the hydrosphere. Many rely on water without understanding the hydrosphere and water cycle. Most people are not aware of the damage they cause to the hydrosphere. People are using up and destroying this valuable **natural resource**.

People use water every day for things such as drinking, bathing, cooking and cleaning. These are direct uses of water. People also use water indirectly. Farmers use water for crops and livestock, which feed people. Companies and factories use water to make products they sell.

People also pollute water, often without understanding the consequences. **Contaminated** water harms life on Earth. Life cannot survive without clean water. Bodies of water are now shrinking, and usable water is becoming scarcer.

natural resource a material found in nature that is useful to people
contaminated unfit for use because of contact with a harmful substance

Surface water is found above the ground. It makes up 0.25 per cent of all the water on Earth. Oceans, lakes and rivers are sources of surface water. People use 1 trillion litres (275 billion gallons) of surface water every day in the United States.

Bodies of water provide people with food. Fishers make their living on the water. Commercial fishing feeds families and communities all around the world. Healthier surface water means a healthier food supply.

Fishing is a common way of making a living along coastlines.

Hydroelectricity is a clean alternative energy source.

Surface water is also used to make power. People build dams to collect water. The trapped water is then channelled through power plants. The waves and currents of this water are moving energy. The moving water turns **turbines** that power generators that make electricity. **Hydroelectricity** powers many homes, towns and cities.

turbine a machine with blades that can be turned by wind, steam or water

hydroelectricity a form of energy caused by flowing water

People also build reservoirs to collect water. Reservoirs are huge human-made lakes that store water. First people use machinery to dig lake basins. Then they use dams to redirect river water. Reservoirs collect water during the rainy season and store it for the dry season. People use the reserves during times of drought. Larger populations have a greater need for reservoirs, especially in dry climates.

Surface water is important to industries worldwide. Most mining and manufacturing businesses use water during production. Factories and refineries often use energy from river water to power machines. Water cools machinery, and high-pressure water cleans it. Water is also used in the products being sold.

Marble-cutting factories use water to cool huge slabs of marble while being cut.

Barges often travel up and down rivers carrying heavy cargo.

Industrial companies use surface water to transport goods. People load boats, barges and ferries with products and ship them all over the world. Travelling by water can be faster and cheaper than ground or air transportation.

HOW PEOPLE USE GROUNDWATER

Groundwater is one of the largest sources of fresh water on Earth. It exists almost everywhere. Rain and melting snow seep into the ground. Groundwater slowly moves through layers of soil, sand and rock. Trillions of litres of groundwater are stored in **aquifers** deep beneath the surface. Some of this water has been underground for millions of years. But these groundwater reserves are shrinking.

FACT

Ice makes up most of Earth's freshwater sources, but 96 per cent of the remaining fresh water is groundwater.

A well supplies a water tank for cattle in Colorado, United States.

aquifer an underground lake or stream of water

In the United Kingdom, people use over 6 million litres (1.6 million gallons) of groundwater every day. Most people never think about groundwater because they cannot see it. Yet it is one of the most used natural resources on the planet. People dig wells in the ground and pump water to the surface. Most groundwater is used for agriculture, communities and households.

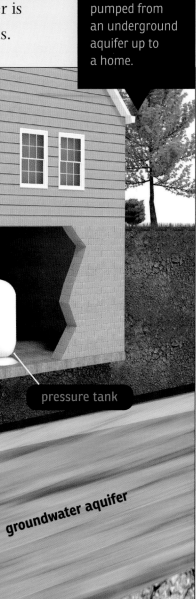

Water is pumped from an underground aquifer up to a home.

well casing

electrical wiring

pressure tank

pump

gravel screen

groundwater aquifer

In many parts of the world, groundwater is important for farming. People depend on farmers to grow food. Irrigating crops and raising livestock requires a lot of water. More than 60 per cent of water used for irrigation comes from underground. In the United States, for example, 204 billion litres (54 billion gallons) of groundwater are used every day just on crops.

Over the whole world, groundwater makes up almost a third of the fresh water available. Almost all the water **consumers** use for farming, industry and drinking has been groundwater at some point. Communities store groundwater for public use. Water towers send water through underground pipes to homes, schools and local businesses.

Automatic irrigation systems are used to water fields.

consumer a person who buys or uses products or services

Water towers hold large quantities of water that gets pumped out to homes and businesses.

Individual families are the third-largest consumers of groundwater. The average US family uses 1,136 litres (300 gallons) of groundwater every day. Most simply have to turn on a tap. Half of the country depends on groundwater for drinking. In **rural** areas, groundwater supplies 99 per cent of the drinking water. People also use groundwater to cook, clean and shower.

FACT

Washing machines and toilets use more water than any other appliance.

rural having to do with the countryside or farming

OVERCONSUMPTION

Water has many uses, but it is not distributed evenly around the world. That's why people collect it, store it and move it. But having that control also makes it easier for people to take more water than they need. Overconsumption disrupts the balance of the entire hydrosphere.

Enough water is not always available for uses such as watering crops.

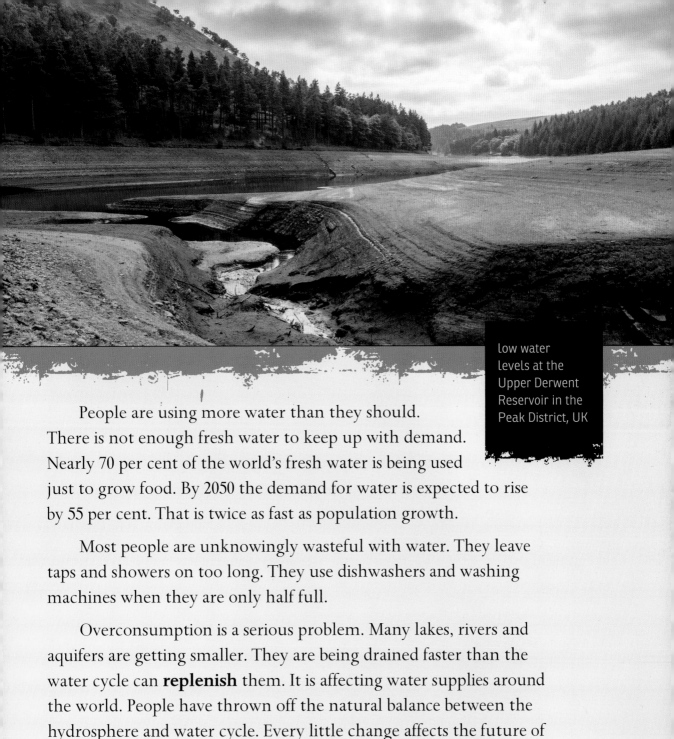

People are using more water than they should.
There is not enough fresh water to keep up with demand.
Nearly 70 per cent of the world's fresh water is being used
just to grow food. By 2050 the demand for water is expected to rise
by 55 per cent. That is twice as fast as population growth.

Most people are unknowingly wasteful with water. They leave
taps and showers on too long. They use dishwashers and washing
machines when they are only half full.

Overconsumption is a serious problem. Many lakes, rivers and
aquifers are getting smaller. They are being drained faster than the
water cycle can **replenish** them. It is affecting water supplies around
the world. People have thrown off the natural balance between the
hydrosphere and water cycle. Every little change affects the future of
water on Earth.

replenish to make full again

Pollution harms the hydrosphere and the environment. Pollutants contaminate water and make it dangerous for plants, animals and people.

Litter is the most obvious form of pollution. Litter is rubbish people leave behind. It floats in water, covers shorelines and gets stuck in sewer drains. Litter can come from people, and it can also come from landfills. Rubbish blows in the wind. It is carried across the countryside and eventually gets trapped in bodies of water.

While some litter, such as food, breaks down, plastics do not.

A crop duster sprays chemicals over a field.

Industrial waste is another form of pollution. Some companies dump harmful chemicals when they have finished using them. The toxic waste seeps into groundwater and flows into oceans.

Farm chemicals also pollute groundwater and surface water. **Fertilizers** and **pesticides** flow with rainwater into streams, rivers and lakes. Runoff pollutes water sources with unnatural nutrients. With the extra nutrients in the water, algae may grow out of control and kill fish.

Pollution and disease

Pollution is a serious problem around the world. Water sources are already extremely polluted in many countries. Polluted water breeds bacteria. It can cause outbreaks of deadly diseases. Waterborne diseases kill 14,000 people across the world every day! Nearly 1.5 billion people do not have access to clean drinking water.

fertilizer a substance added to soil to make crops grow better

pesticide a poisonous chemical used to kill pests such as insects, rats and fungi that can damage plants

21

Oil spills are another form of pollution caused by people. People mine oil to use as an energy source. Huge oil reserves are found at the bottom of the ocean. Oil companies build large drilling rigs in the ocean to extract the oil. Pipes sometimes break and spill oil into the water. Oil floats on the surface and spreads quickly. It is hard to contain and even harder to clean up. The greasy pollutant sticks to everything. Oil contaminates water, kills marine animals and destroys shorelines.

Crews work to clean up an oil spill in Ao Prao Beach at Samet Island.

Oil spills affect animals such as birds, fish and other ocean wildlife.

GLOBAL WARMING

People turn mined oil into petrol. Petrol is burned to fuel cars, and cars pollute the air with exhaust smoke. Smoke is filled with the harmful greenhouse gas, carbon dioxide. Greenhouse gases trap heat in the atmosphere. They are responsible for **global warming**.

atmosphere

Sun

solar
radiation

Earth

Global warming has a huge impact on water. Trapped heat warms the planet. Higher temperatures speed up the water cycle, and water evaporates faster. Clouds have less time to travel before heavy rains fall. Water is falling back to Earth in the same place where it evaporated. This changes the distribution of water in the hydrosphere. Wet climates are flooding, and dry climates are experiencing droughts and wildfires.

Global warming is melting Earth's glacial ice. Ice is the second-largest water source in the hydrosphere. It is frozen fresh water. It would turn salty if it melted into the ocean.

Some greenhouse gases occur naturally, but human-made greenhouse gases create a harmful, unbalanced amount in the atmosphere.

global warming the idea that Earth's temperature is slowly rising

Sea levels would rise by 70 metres (230 feet) if all the ice melted. Islands and coastlines would be underwater. Hundreds of millions of people would be homeless and forced to move inland. There would be less land to grow crops and raise livestock.

The Muir Glacier in Alaska slowly melted between 1899 to 2003.

Ice Sheet

Ice sheets alone hold 99 per cent of the fresh water on the planet. They form in polar regions that are flat and high in elevation. The two polar ice sheets on Earth today cover Greenland and Antarctica. They store enormous amounts of water. Ice sheets grow when more snow falls than melts. The weight slowly changes the snow from powder to hard ice crystals. Layers of ice compact and get denser over thousands of years. They eventually turn into solid ice. Ice sheets move like liquid water — although much more slowly — and greatly impact the landscape. They shift and slide over everything in their paths. Ice sheets cover entire mountains, valleys and plains.

HOW CAN HUMANS HELP?

The hydrosphere sustains all life on Earth. What people put in the water and how they use it affects the future of the entire planet. Many people may not realize how important water is until it's gone. Water is required for life. People, plants and animals cannot survive without it.

A crew works to clean up litter from a beach in Thailand.

Populations around the world need to work together to save Earth's water. The only **sustainable** solution is to use less water and clean up pollution. Here are a few ways you can help. Turn off taps and take shorter showers. Encourage your family, friends and neighbours to save water too. Recycle bottles, cans, metals, papers and cardboard. Making these small changes will lessen the amount of rubbish in landfills and in the water. Buying organic food and natural products will also help the hydrosphere. It will reduce chemical runoff that flows into drinking water. The choices you make every day affect the future of the hydrosphere.

sustainable done in a way that can be continued and that doesn't use up natural resources

The first public flushing toilets are introduced in Crystal Palace in London.

1851

1858

July and August are known as the Great Stink due to the highly polluted River Thames. Joseph Bazalgette, chief engineer of the Metropolitan Board of Works, develops a new network of sewers to reflow London's existing sewers.

The United Kingdom begins using oil and natural gas found below the North Sea as fuel sources.

1960s

1967

The *Torrey Canyon* spills an estimated 94.6–136 million litres (25–36 million gallons) of oil off the southwest coast of the United Kingdom. The coastlines of Britain, France, Guernsey and Spain are affected.

Oil tanker *Amoco Cadiz* runs aground and sinks. Over one and a half million barrels of oil are spilled into the English Channel near Brittany, France.

1978

1996

The Environment Act of 1996 establishes the Environment Agency (EA) in England and Wales.

GLOSSARY

aquifer an underground lake or stream of water

consumer a person who buys or uses products or services

contaminated unfit for use because of contact with a harmful substance

evaporate to change from a liquid into a vapour or gas

fertilizer a substance added to soil to make crops grow better

global warming the idea that Earth's temperature is slowly rising

hydroelectricity a form of energy caused by flowing water

natural resource a material found in nature that is useful to people

pesticide a poisonous chemical used to kill pests such as insects, rats and fungi that can damage plants

replenish to make full again

reservoir a natural or artificial holding area for storing large amounts of water

rural having to do with the countryside or farming

sustainable done in a way that can be continued and that doesn't use up natural resources

turbine a machine with blades that can be turned by wind, steam or water

water cycle how water changes as it travels around the world and moves between the ground and the air

FIND OUT MORE

Can the Earth Cope?: Water Supply, Louise Spilsbury
(Wayland, 2013)

Saving Water, Jen Green (Wayland, 2014)

Saving Water (First Facts: Water in Our World), Rebecca Olien
(Raintree, 2017)

WEBSITES

www.bbc.co.uk/education/clips/zh3mpv4
Visit this BBC website to watch a video clip explaining how oil
spills damage the environment.

climatekids.nasa.gov/india-groundwater/
Find out how scientists use satellites to monitor supplies
of groundwater.

**science.howstuffworks.com/environmental/earth/geophysics/
h2o6.htm**
Visit this website to find out more about the water cycle.

COMPREHENSION QUESTIONS

- Explain how water moves through the water cycle.

- People pollute water sources through the use of fertilizers and pesticides. What are fertilizers and pesticides?

- What are some effects of global warming?

INDEX